ARE YOU THERE GOD?
IT'S ME, MARGARITA

ARE YOU THERE GOD? IT'S ME, MARGARITA

More Cocktails with a Literary Twist

Tim Federle

Illustrated by Lauren Mortimer
Cocktail Consultant: Cody Goldstein

RUNNING PRESS
PHILADELPHIA

Running Press
Hachette Book Group
1290 Avenue of the Americas,
New York, NY 10104
www.runningpress.com
@Running_Press

Printed in China

First Edition: October 2018

Published by Running Press, an imprint of Perseus Books, LLC,
a subsidiary of Hachette Book Group, Inc. The Running Press
name and logo is a trademark of the Hachette Book Group.

The Hachette Speakers Bureau provides a wide range
of authors for speaking events. To find out more, go to
www.hachettespeakersbureau.com or call (866) 376-6591.

The publisher is not responsible for websites (or their content)
that are not owned by the publisher.

Print book cover and interior design by Josh McDonnell.

Library of Congress Control Number: 2017964321

ISBNs: 978-0-7624-6415-9 (hardcover), 978-0-7624-6414-2 (ebook)

RRD-S   641.87

10 9 8 7 6 5 4 3 2 1

BAR MENU

INTRODUCTION 1

TOOLS. 3
Glassware 3
Equipment 5

TECHNIQUES. 7
Making a Drink 7
Decorating a Drink 9

TERMS. 10
Spirits. 10
Liqueurs and Aperitifs. 11
Beer 12
Wine 12
Other Flavorings 13

PART I:
OLD-SCHOOL SIPS 17
Tender Is the Nightcap 18
Portrait of the Artist as a Drunk Man 20
The Island of Dr. Merlot 23
The Grappa of Wrath 25
She Stoops to Cointreau 26
Murder on the Orient Espresso 29
The Greyhound of the Baskervilles 30
Billy Budd Light 33
The Tequila Sun Also Rises 35
The Canterbury Ales. 36
Madame Brewery. 39
Of Mice and Manischewitz 41

Lord Jim Beam 42

Dangerous Libations. 44

The Brothers Kamikaze 47

A Room with Vermouth 49

As I Lay Drinking 50

The Call of the Wild Turkey 53

Absolut, Absolut! 54

David Copper Mug. 55

PART II:

CONTEMPORARY COCKTAILS. 57

The Handmaid's Ale 58

Fifty Shades of Grey Goose 60

Extremely Drunk and Incredibly Close 63

Rabbit, Rum 65

The Hard Cider House Rules. 66

A Heartbreaking Work of Staggering Guinness 68

Go Get a Scotch, Man. 69

Nineteen Eighty-Forty 70

Drinker Tailor Soldier Spy 73

The Drinking Game of Thrones 75

Gin and the Art of Motorcycle Maintenance. . . 76

The Wine of Beauty 79

The Hitchhiker's Mudslide to the Galaxy 81

Muddlesex. 82

The Bellini Jar 84

The Amazing Adventures of
    Have a Beer and Stay. 87

A Time to Swill 88

Are You There God? It's Me, Margarita 90

The Bluest Mai Tai 91

PART III:

VIRGINAL VOLUMES 93

The Wine in the Willows 95

Lord of the Pimms. 96

Long Island, the Witch, and the Wardrobe 99

Watership Down the Hatch 101

Little Soused on the Prairie 102

Frog and Toad Are Sober. 103

Goodnight Moonshine 104

Caps for Ale 106

The Berenstain Beers 107

The Seagram's Garden 108

PART IV:

SCHOLARLY SNACKS. 111

Animal Crackers Farm 113

Salads for Algernon 115

The Curious Incident of the
   Hot Dog in the Nighttime 117

The Fridges of Madison County. 118

War and Peas. 121

Banana Karenina 122

BONUS! DRINKING GAME 123

FORMULAS FOR METRIC CONVERSION 125

ACKNOWLEDGMENTS 126

INDEX. 127

INTRODUCTION

Books, meet booze.

Dear librarians and lushes—and everyone in between,

A toast to you! You've whipped through *Fifty Shades of Grey*, quested across *Lord of the Rings*, and said "Goodnight" to so many moons, you're practically an astronaut. Could anyone blame you if all those pages left you a little parched?

Welcome to *Are You There God? It's Me, Margarita*.

Around here, there's always a stool with your name on it—and we'll never (library) card you. But fear not—you don't have to be an English major to drink your way through this all-new cocktail guide! *Are You There God? It's Me, Margarita* is for recovering readers as much as it is for beginning bartenders, with a drink or three to suit all tastes.

For classic cocktail hounds and fans of bygone books, we've got tasty new twists on everything from Moscow mules (served in a David Copper Mug, natch) to elevated staples (The Brothers Kamikaze) and even to wildly sweet wines (Of Mice and Manischewitz, anyone?). Our Old-School Sips section celebrates everything both timeworn and tasty.

For contemporary cocktail enthusiasts and first-in-line fans of new releases, we're serving mashed-up modern masterpieces (hello, Muddlesex), goblet-worthy guzzlers (good evening, The Drinking Game of Thrones), and drinks so out of this world,

1

they're practically comical (strap yourself in for The Hitchhiker's Mudslide to the Galaxy). Our Contemporary Cocktails section is hot off the press and chilled to the last drop.

And for all you designated drivers out there, we're picking up your tab, too. Our nonalcoholic drinks, inspired by the books that defined your childhood, are bound to get you a Little Soused on the Prairie—at least in spirit, if not *spirits*.

When it's break time in this bookstore, take off your reading glasses and bring on the snacks. Our Banana Karenina is so delicious, you'll swear you're cheating—on your diet!

If you're newer to a mixing glass than you are to the masterworks, see facing page to breeze through our bartender crash course. For now, and without further ado, let's bookmark some booze and stir up some books. After all, even if you don't own the collected works of Shakespeare, tonight you're gonna drink like you do.

TOOLS

Glassware

Collins Glass (10 to 14 ounces): Built like a highball glass, but taller and narrower. Best for icy, very large tropical drinks. Lord Jim Beam, anyone?

Copper Mug (10 to 12 ounces): Every Instagram post of a Moscow mule features one of these, but around here we mix it up with drinks that step outside the vodka box. David Copper Mug, you're on.

Coupe Glass (5 to 7 ounces): How the English do Champagne —and how hipsters drink it these days. Elegant but low-key, with a rounded bowl.

Highball (10 to 12 ounces): Midway between a rocks and a Collins glass, but taller than the former and shorter and fatter than the latter. If you could only have one book on a desert island, you'd choose wisely; if you could only have one glass, you'd choose this.

Mason Jar (1 cup to ½ gallon): Though generally used for bottling preserves, this also makes for a great drink vessel. Get ready for a whole lotta Southern stories served up farm-style.

Mug (10 to 12 ounces): This hardworking coffee cup does double duty for hot alcoholic drinks. If you thought *Fifty Shades of Grey* steamed up your Kindle, wait'll you try some of our piping-hot hooch.

Pint Glass (16 to 20 ounces): An all-purpose beer-chugger, this glass tapers at the bottom, and some of them have a "bulb" near the lip for a better grip.

Rocks (or Lowball or Old-Fashioned) Glass (6 to 10 ounces): A drink poured "on the rocks"—that's over ice, rookie—is frequently served in one of these short, heavy tumblers.

Shot Glass (¾ to 2 ounces): For enjoying a variety of aptly named "shots." The smallest of drinking vessels, these are also handy as measuring devices.

Thermos (up to 40 ounces): A go-to container for on-the-go readers. (Note: Never drink and drive, but *do* put on an audiobook and coast.)

Wineglass (8 to 22 ounces): With as many subtle shapes as there are types of wine (and genres of book), we put the wineglass to work on drinks that go beyond your basic Bordeaux.

Equipment

Jigger: For small liquid measurements. Made out of metal in an hourglass shape, it's available in a variety of sizes. We prefer the 1-ounce over the 1½-ounce model.

Juicer: The classy crowd prefers their lemons and limes freshly juiced, whether by hand or by machine—but we won't balk if you go the bottled route. On average, lemons and limes produce about an ounce of juice each.

Measuring Cups and Spoons: Dry cups typically range from ¼ cup to 1 cup. For larger liquid measurements, it's easiest to have a standard 2-cup glass measuring cup. Measuring spoons range in size from ¼ teaspoon to 1 tablespoon.

Muddler: Grown-up term for a fruit masher, which looks like a mini baseball bat. Releases oils and flavors in herbs and berries.

Shaker: An essential device that need not intimidate. Our fave is the *Cobbler*—a three-part metal contraption (counting the capped lid) with the strainer built right in. The other varieties are the *Boston* (a glass mixing cup and metal container) and the *French* (basically a Cobbler shaker sans strainer). Both require a separate strainer, and that's valuable time you could be hanging out at the library. Or writing the next great American novel. Or drinking.

Strainer: Like a sifter for liquids. If you ignored our advice to buy the all-in-one Cobbler shaker, you'll want to pick up a Hawthorne strainer, which will fit tightly into your shaker's metal mouth. The Hawthorne filters only the liquids (not the ice) into a cocktail.

Vegetable Peeler: A handy tool for creating twists (see Garnishes, page 9), the peeler removes a thin layer of skin from fruit to add flavor and color.

TECHNIQUES

Making a Drink

Double-Straining: For some recipes, you'll hold a mesh strainer over the mouth of the glass and "double-strain" the drink from the shaker through a strainer and then through the mesh. Makes for an ultra-clean pour.

Dry-Shaking: Same thing as Shaking (page 8), but without the addition of ice to the shaker.

Dumping: After shaking your ingredients, uncap the shaker and "dump" all that's inside—including, generally, the ice—as opposed to straining through a filter. (The cocktail equivalent of turning in the first draft of a manuscript that hasn't been edited.)

Filling: In some recipes, you're asked to "fill" your glass to the top with a final ingredient—typically Champagne, soda, or cream. The amount of liquid needed depends on how large your glass is: from 2 to 4 ounces for a flute, to anywhere from 4 to 8 ounces for rocks, highball, or Collins glasses.

Muddling: In some recipes, once you've filled a glass with the specified fruits, juices, or herbs, use a muddler (page 5) to gently mash the ingredients, twisting lightly to release oils and flavors.

Rimming: Rub the lip of the desired glass with a lemon or lime wedge, then "rim" the glass by turning it upside down and placing the rim on a plate of salt, Tang powder, sugar, or whatever the recipe calls for. Then gently rotate the glass so the rim gets coated in the desired ingredient.

Shaking: Fill a Cobbler tin with all the ingredients and ice, close the cap, and shake vigorously until the liquid takes on a foamy quality. Take off the lid and strain (or Dump, see page 7) into a glass.

Stirring: Experts use a bar spoon, which has a long, twisting handle, but an everyday spoon will do just fine. For cocktails with carbonation, the bubbles do the stirring for you.

Decorating a Drink

Garnishes: These add both color and flavor (like a lime wedge or a lemon twist). Think of adverbs as the garnish of prose—especially when your editor makes you cut them. Ruthlessly.

Garnishing techniques include:

Grating: Not just for cheese! Gently rub the desired ingredient (lemon peel, ginger) against the fine edge of a grater.

Twists: Delicately flavor a drink and add a little citrus pizzazz. Our preferred method is to wash a lemon and then use a *vegetable peeler* to remove a 2-inch strip of rind. Fold in half, twist over the drink, wipe the rim of the glass with the twist, and then drop the twist into the glass.

Wedges: The most widely seen lemon or lime garnishes. Wash, dry, and cut the ends off the whole fruit. Then chop the fruit in half "the short way" and quarter the remaining halves. Wedges can either be squeezed and dropped into the drink, or balanced on the rim after cutting a notch into the fruit. Kind of like a bookmark for a drink.

Wheels: Circular discs of fruits or vegetables. Wash, dry, and cut the ends off the whole fruit, then slice crosswise into "wheels." Can be placed in the drink, or balanced on the rim after cutting a notch into the fruit.

TERMS

Spirits

Gin: Distilled from grain and can be flavored with everything from juniper to cinnamon. Look for its star appearance in *The Great Gatsby*. But only after you've finished reading *this* book.

Rum: The best sugar-water money can buy. The lightest kinds are the youngest; the darkest can be older than seven years. Keep this away from Hemingway, thank you.

Tequila: Comes from the blue agave plant, not the cactus. The word "tequila" itself refers to a very specific region in Mexico, and the authentic stuff doesn't harbor any wayward worms.

Vodka: Odorless and clear, vodka is typically distilled from potatoes and grains. Pairs best with Russian classics.

Whiskey: Distilled from grains and hailing from America, Canada, Ireland, or Scotland. An acquired taste, to some—but aren't the best books, too?

Liqueurs and Aperitifs

Strong, syrupy spirits that are flavored any number of ways, from fruits to flowers; also includes schnapps. The following liqueurs make appearances throughout this book: *bitter orange* (brands like Campari and Aperol), *blackcurrant* (aka, crème de cassis), *coffee* (a brand like Kahlúa), *crème de cacao* (chocolate flavor), *elderflower* (a brand like St-Germain), *ginger* (a brand like Domaine de Canton), *hazelnut* (a brand like Frangelico), *Irish coffee*, *orange* (generics like triple sec; brands like Cointreau and Grand Marnier), *ouzo* and *pastis* (licorice flavor).

Beer

A malt brew and a hoppy flavor. Recipes in this book focus on ales, stouts, and pilsners. And, like the best genre-busting novels (yes, you, *In Cold Blood*), our beer cocktails go beyond the pint glass to mix flavors (and break rules).

Wine

Fermented juice from myriad fruits, especially grapes. In subcategories, we feature *brandy*, generally a distillation of wine or fruit juice; *sweet vermouth*, a fortified wine flavored with herbs; *sherry*, a brightly sweet fortified wine hailing from Spain; and *Champagne*, a sparkling white wine from a specific French region.

Other Flavorings

Activated Charcoal: Get thee to your local health food store. A highly absorbent powdered form of every dad's favorite BBQ staple.

Aquafaba: An egg substitute most easily obtained by draining the liquid from canned chickpeas.

Bitters: The cologne of cocktails, added in small amounts to give a drink depth and nuance. Those featured in this book range from chocolate mole to baked apple to the more standard Angostura bitters.

Blue Pea Flower: Bright, beautiful, and straight-up Insta-worthy, find this one in the tea aisle.

Cinnamon Syrup: They pump it behind the counter at Starbucks, but ours is a cinch to make at home.

CINNAMON SYRUP

In a small saucepan, heat 1 cup each of water and brown sugar, and 2 teaspoons powdered cinnamon, and whisk until mixed. Bring to a boil and then reduce heat, continuing to whisk until you've got syrup. Pour into a mason jar, add ½ teaspoon vanilla syrup, and keep bottled for about 3 to 4 weeks.

Clamato: A branded beverage; don't try this one at home, unless you've got a bunch of clams and tomatoes sitting around. In which case: Who are you, Huck Finn?

Grenadine: A sweet red syrup that's a snap to make, and loads better than the corporate high-fructose junk sold to bars.

GRENADINE SYRUP

Boil 2 cups bottled pomegranate juice (a brand like POM Wonderful) with 2 cups granulated sugar in a medium saucepan. Stir for 5 minutes, until it's reduced to half its original volume and turns into a syrup. Bottle and keep in the fridge for 2 months.

Hemp Milk: Peace, man! No cows were harmed in the making of this "milk," which is really a watery concoction made from soaking hemp seeds.

Lapsang Souchong Tea: A black tea from China known for its smoked-wood flavor.

Orgeat Syrup: A fancy-schmancy almond syrup frequently used in French-Polynesian drinks. *South Pacific*? More like *soused* Pacific. (I'll see myself out.)

Peach Puree: A staple for bellinis. Place 1 diced peach, 1 tablespoon lemon juice, and half a pinch of sugar in a food processor; blend until smooth.

Sake: A Japanese alcoholic beverage, served both hot and cold, made from fermented rice.

Simple Syrup: Avoid the high-fructose junk bottled by the gallon. For easy, at-home simple syrup, boil 1 part water to 2 parts sugar, until it reduces to—you guessed it—syrup. Place in a bottle with a tight-fitting cap, refrigerate, and enjoy within a month.

Sour Mix: Steer clear of the grocery aisle. For our recipes, combine half an ounce each of fresh lemon juice, lime juice, and simple syrup.

Tang: A throwback powdered drink mix made famous by NASA in the 1960s.

Yuzu Juice: A bottled Japanese citrus juice, found at your local specialty grocer.

Thirsty yet? Put down the book and pick up a shaker. These recipes aren't going to make themselves!

PART I

OLD-SCHOOL SIPS

"I drink to make other people more interesting."

—ERNEST HEMINGWAY

Attention, freshmen! Time to brush up on those twenty-pound books you long ago dragged across the quad. With so many classics asking weighty questions about life (paging Fyodor Dostoyevsky), love (I'm lookin' at you, *She Stoops to Conquer*), and men lost at sea (too many to count), you could use a stiff drink. We're as serious about drinks as your Russian lit prof was about Chekhov—but how about trading in Solo cups for something a tad classier? Read on and drink up.

TENDER IS THE NIGHTCAP

Tender Is the Night (1934)

by F. Scott Fitzgerald

This is arguably the work closest to the author's heart. Fitzgerald himself was said to have written to a friend: "If you liked *The Great Gatsby*, for God sake read this. *Gatsby* was a tour de force but this is a confession of faith." (Or, as we'd say today: "Five stars out of five; would recommend.") Set on the French Riviera with a cast of teen starlets (meet Rosemary), philandering psychiatrists (hi, Dick), and women on the verge of a nervous breakdown (poor Nicole), *Tender Is the Night* echoed the very themes that haunted Fitzgerald's own life story. Step away from your entanglements with a Riviera-worthy "Rosemary" spritz.

> 2 ounces Aperol
>
> 1 rosemary sprig, plus 1 additional sprig with stem, for garnish
>
> 3 ounces prosecco
>
> 4 ounces club soda

Place the Aperol and rosemary sprig in a wineglass and muddle—*tenderly*, of course. Add the prosecco and club soda over ice and garnish with an additional on-stem rosemary sprig.

PORTRAIT OF THE ARTIST AS A DRUNK MAN

Portrait of the Artist as a Young Man (1916)
by James Joyce

For any reader choosing between a life devoted to either the priesthood or art—and really, who isn't?—*Portrait* will resonate mightily. Employing a nifty stream-of-consciousness narrative, Joyce's first published work follows young Stephen from age five all the way to when he decides to flee home, with each chapter's reading level increasing in complexity right alongside Stephen's own life predicaments. Whether you're the praying kind or not, this nutty-flavored cocktail from a friar-shaped bottle will have you on your knees.

> 2 ounces Irish whiskey
> 2 ounces hazelnut liqueur (like Frangelico)
> 1 ounce Baileys

Pour all ingredients into a rocks glass over ice. Then count your blessings—and stir your drink.

THE ISLAND OF DR. MERLOT

The Island of Dr. Moreau (1896)

by H. G. Wells

Though this classic has been in print for over a century, and inspired no less than five feature-film adaptations, author H. G. Wells wasn't even aware that he was writing science fiction. He preferred the term "scientific romances" (which is exactly what I call a night on Tinder). Speaking of monstrous half-animals: This book finds our narrator shipwrecked on an island devoted to the devious deeds of one Dr. Moreau, whose idea of a good time is playing Frankenstein with creature-slash-human-hybrid experiments. Throw your own luau with a Merlot-based island cocktail that'll have you howling at the moon.

2 ounces Merlot

2 ounces pineapple juice

2 ounces simple syrup (page 15)

½ ounce orange juice

¼ ounce lime juice

Bacon, for garnish

Pour all the liquid ingredients into a mixing glass with ice. Stir for 10 seconds and then strain into a wineglass over fresh ice. Garnish with a piece of bacon.

THE GRAPPA OF WRATH

The Grapes of Wrath (1939)

by John Steinbeck

Though it won the Pulitzer for fiction in 1940, these *Grapes* left half their readers sour, with calls to ban the book over Steinbeck's allegedly communist leanings. Of course, when it wasn't being burned, banned, or booed, the book's unsentimental portrayal of America during the Great Depression inspired no less than Eleanor Roosevelt to call for a closer examination of migrant camps. Our farmer-worthy lemonade with a hint of Grappa is a toast to every high school teacher who ever assigned it—and every student who skipped the SparkNotes and actually read it.

2 ounces Grappa

2 ounces lemon juice

2 ounces simple syrup (page 15)

1 ounce grape juice

5 frozen grapes

Club soda, to fill

Pour all the liquid ingredients into a shaker with ice and shake for 5 seconds. Strain into a Collins glass over the frozen grapes, top with the soda, and prepare for a wrath of deliciousness.

SHE STOOPS TO COINTREAU

She Stoops to Conquer (1773)
by Oliver Goldsmith

If you've ever played dumb to win over an easily intimidated guy, (a) stop that right now! and (b) welcome to the plot of this classic play. First staged at the Covent Garden Theatre in the eighteenth century, and still widely performed today, this Restoration comedy of manners finds two eligible bachelors hoodwinked into thinking they're spending the evening at an inn (it's actually a house). Comedy and chaos ensue, with our title character ("She") pretending to be a bar wench ("stoops") in order to see the true colors of her man ("to conquer"). Mix ingredients both highbrow and low for a beverage that'll have your suitor standing up straight.

1 ounce Cointreau
1 ounce sour mix (page 15)
1 teaspoon granulated sugar
3 ounces Champagne

Pour the Cointreau, sour mix, and sugar into a rocks glass, and muddle till dissolved. Add a scoop of ice, pour the Champagne, and conquer that thirst.

MURDER ON THE
ORIENT ESPRESSO

Murder on the Orient Express (1934)
by Agatha Christie

Agatha Christie's final public appearance—on the red carpet of the first *Orient Express* film adaptation in 1974—occurred forty years after the book debuted in six installments of the *Saturday Evening Post*. Christie was said to have traveled aboard the real train over sixty times, beginning with a solo trip in the 1920s. Her glamorous, compulsively readable account of a Belgian detective tracking down a murderer aboard a snowed-in train reads like *Clue* on a choo-choo train—with a last-minute detour. (Spoiler alert: They *all* dun-it.) Our tipsy, Belgian-inspired espresso will have you wide-eyed and solving crimes before you get too far off track.

> 1 ounce coffee liqueur (like Kahlúa)
> 4 ounces hot coffee
> 2 shots espresso
> 1 ounce simple syrup (page 15)
> 1 piece Belgian chocolate, for garnish

Pour all the liquid ingredients into a mug and float the Belgian chocolate on top. Now go find a seat in the quiet car and enjoy.

THE GREYHOUND OF THE BASKERVILLES

The Hound of the Baskervilles (1902)

by Sir Arthur Conan Doyle

A prequel of sorts, this haunted hound howled onto the scene nearly a decade after Sir Arthur killed Sherlock Holmes by pushing him off a cliff in *The Final Problem*. Despite Conan Doyle's wish for his more "serious" fiction to be taken, well, more seriously, this return of Sherlock proved such a hit that he brought the crime-fighter back for good—along with the ever-wise Watson, who figured prominently in this ghoulish tale of ghost dogs. Put down your pipe for a smoked-salt Greyhound that's so delicious, it's criminal.

> Smoked sea salt, for cocktail rim (page 8)
> Chipotle pepper flakes, for cocktail rim (page 8)
> 2 ounces British gin (like Beefeater)
> 4 ounces grapefruit juice
> 1 teaspoon hot sauce

Rim a Collins glass with the salt and pepper flakes, add ice and the liquid ingredients, and stir. *Who drunk it?* Don't look at me!

BILLY BUDD LIGHT

Billy Budd (1924)

by Herman Melville

Helpful tip: If you don't want your diaries published, burn them before you head to the great bar in the sky (or throw your phone into the nearest ocean). Although Melville is best known for his classic whale tale (I'm lookin' at you, *Moby-Dick*!), he had been relegated to the footnotes of literature before his eventual biographer uncovered the unpublished *Billy Budd* manuscript over thirty years after his death. Melville had a thing for the high seas, and *Budd*, written during his final years, is a tragedy about an innocent sailor accused of a crime he didn't commit. Find your land legs again before pouring yourself this brawny beer beverage with a sea-foam finish.

> 2 ounces clamato (page 14)
> 1 ounce aquafaba (page 13)
> ½ ounce salted water
> Bud Light, to fill

Pour the clamato, aquafaba, and salted water into a shaker. Dry-shake, without ice, for 10 seconds. Pour into a pint glass and top with Bud Light. Land (*hiccup*) ho!

THE TEQUILA SUN ALSO RISES

The Sun Also Rises (1926)

by Ernest Hemingway

Picture yourself in post–World War I Paris, but don't get too comfy; why sit back in the city of lights when you could be running from the bulls in nearby Spain? That's not all our tragic leading man Jake is running from, however. In *The Sun Also Rises*, an unnamed war injury leaves our hero unable to perform in the bedroom, despite his having the hots for a volatile and newly single British babe. This allegorical novel put Hemingway on the map as a major voice of Americana. Our Spanish-themed twist on a tequila sunrise will have you going from *hola* to *olé* in two shakes.

> 1 ½ ounces tequila
> 4 ounces orange juice
> ½ ounce grenadine (page 14)
> 1 ounce Rioja wine

Pour the tequila, orange juice, and grenadine into a Collins glass over ice. Slowly pour the Rioja on top to float, and saddle up for a no-bull beverage.

THE CANTERBURY ALES

The Canterbury Tales (1476)
by Geoffrey Chaucer

Before "One hundred bottles of beer on the wall"; before license plate games; before asking Dad to pull over to pee after only ten minutes on the highway—there was *The Canterbury Tales*. Written in regular old English (and not, *Gasp!*, Latin) in the fourteenth century, this trailblazing book follows a group of pilgrims on a journey to a Canterbury cathedral, with each traveler challenged to outdo one another—and help pass the time—with their own tale well told. (They apparently didn't have podcasts back then.) Stock up on your next quest with this trail mix tipple people will be telling stories about.

6 ounces pale ale

1 ounce hazelnut liqueur (like Frangelico)

4 ounces prune juice

1 pinch salt

1 teaspoon chocolate sauce

Pretzel, for garnish

Place all ingredients, except for the pretzel, in a Thermos (or pint glass) and stir. Garnish with a pretzel on top, take a sip, and look for a rest stop.

MADAME BREWERY

Madame Bovary (1856)
by Gustave Flaubert

Title character Emma Bovary (or *Madame*, if you're nasty) proved such a pivot away from "demure" nineteenth-century female characters that author Gustave Flaubert was put on trial for writing obscenity. (He was eventually acquitted, which did wonders for sales.) Concerning a doctor's wife who finds herself cheating in order to *feel* something again, this book's most famous scene involves a horse-drawn carriage that's *still* raising eyebrows and temperatures (*giddyup!*). You'll do your own panting for our "medicinal" bitters with a French-brewed twist.

> 3 ounces stout beer
> ½ ounce pastis
> 3 dashes Angostura bitters
> 3 ounces cold (or cold brew) coffee
> Lemon twist, for garnish

Pour all liquid ingredients into a French press, press down once to mix, and pour over ice in a rocks glass. Garnish with a lemon twist. *Ooh-la-lush*!

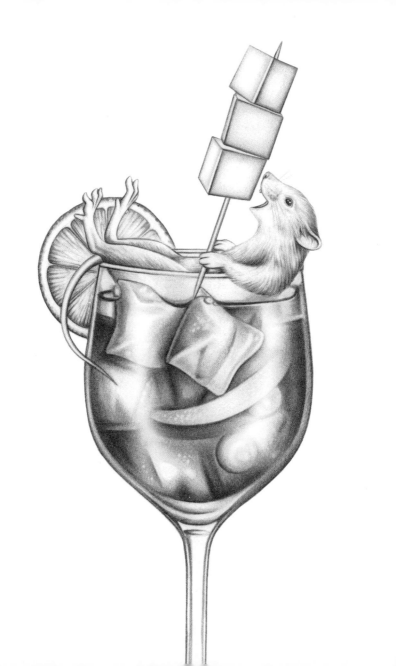

OF MICE AND MANISCHEWITZ

Of Mice and Men (1937)

by John Steinbeck

Forget excuses about your homework—Steinbeck's dog literally ate the *entire handwritten first draft* of this eventual classic, sending him back to page one before delivering a book whose first edition would go on to sell half a million copies. Originally a novella before being adapted into a knockout stage play (and a bunch of film adaptations), *Mice* tells the Depression-era story of childhood friends: one who is kind and loyal and the other a giant who tragically doesn't know his own strength. Who's the mouse and who's the man? You decide. Beat your own great depressions with our farm-fresh sangria.

> 4 ounces Manischewitz red wine
>
> 1 ounce simple syrup (page 15)
>
> 2 apples, washed and sliced
>
> 2 oranges, in segments
>
> 15 blueberries
>
> 3 small squares cheddar cheese, for garnish

Combine the Manischewitz, syrup, and fruits in a small pitcher with ice, and stir. Pour into a wineglass over ice and garnish with three toothpick-skewered cubes of cheese. It's quittin' time!

LORD JIM BEAM

Lord Jim (1900)
by Joseph Conrad

From Herman Melville to Jules Verne, writers of yesteryear loved to send their men out to sea—and then churn the waters. Conrad is no exception, and though critics initially dismissed this former seaman's work as waterlogged, teachers are still assigning *Lord Jim* today. Based on a true story about a sinking ship abandoned by its crew, this timeless tale of guilt, redemption, and shipwrecks asks difficult questions about how you'd react in do-or-die situations. (Hint: Throw a life preserver before grabbing your own floatie.) Bust out a tiki torch for this tropical cocktail that's fit for a captain—whether or not he actually deserves it.

2 ounces Jim Beam bourbon

2 ounces pineapple juice

1 ounce cinnamon syrup (page 14)

1 ounce orgeat syrup

½ ounce lime juice

Cinnamon stick, for garnish

Combine all liquid ingredients in a shaker with ice, shake for 5 seconds, and double-strain into a tiki mug (or a Collins glass) over ice. Light a cinnamon stick on fire (think *Survivor*), blow it out so it glows like a smoke signal, and drop it into the drink to garnish.

DANGEROUS LIBATIONS

Dangerous Liaisons (1782)
by Pierre Choderlos de Laclos

Before it was a late-eighties Oscar-winner starring Glenn Close, John Malkovich, and Michelle Pfeiffer, *Dangerous*'s danger-doing characters appeared in a stage adaptation inspired by the scandalously sexy 1700s-era novel. If you've ever hidden the cover of *Fifty Shades of Grey* while riding public transportation, you'll relate to this book's most *Dangerous* readers—including none other than Marie Antoinette, who couldn't get enough of its lusting lovers. A story told entirely in scorching-hot letters, you'll savor this inky-black drink that's *dangerous* till the last drop.

1 ounce crème de cassis

1 ounce lemon juice

1 teaspoon activated charcoal (optional, for color)

4 ounces Champagne

Combine the crème de cassis, lemon juice, and activated charcoal in a shaker with ice and shake for 5 seconds. Strain into a coupe glass, top with Champagne, and share with your (nearest) lover.

THE BROTHERS KAMIKAZE

The Brothers Karamazov (1880)

by Fyodor Dostoyevsky

Nothing tests a family like a good old-fashioned fight over a will (enter: the brothers Karamazov). Widely considered one of the finest novels of all time, Dostoyevsky's final work asks all the big questions—*What is the meaning of life? And can I please borrow three thousand rubles??*—and offers no easy answers. If you think the themes are heavy, try picking up this eight-hundred-plus-page tome without bending from the knees. A drink or several should help; you'll be fighting over three takes on one classic kamikaze.

Brother one
1 ounce vodka
1 ounce triple sec
1 ounce lime juice

Brother three
1 ounce vodka
1 ounce Cointreau
1 ounce grapefruit juice

Brother two
1 ounce vodka
1 ounce orange juice
1 ounce lemon juice

For each recipe: Pour the ingredients into a shaker with ice and shake for 3 seconds. Strain each into its own shot glass, bro.

A ROOM WITH VERMOUTH

A Room with a View (1908)
by E. M. Forster

If you've ever arrived at a hotel only to discover that your room with a "view" is of a parking lot, welcome to the opening scene of E. M. Forster's beloved novel, the first he began writing and the third to be published. Considered Forster's lightest work, *Room* lets you settle in for a view of Florentine vistas and sidekick spinsters, all while questioning how one does and doesn't fit into society's preordained pecking order. As for you, you'll fit in just fine as soon as you serve your suitor this drink, which boasts a taste of Italy and a view of the blue sky.

> 2 ounces dry vermouth
> 1 ounce blue curaçao
> 1 ounce lemon juice
> 1 ounce simple syrup (page 15)
> 1 egg white

Pour the vermouth, curaçao, lemon juice, syrup, and egg white into a shaker and dry-shake, for 5 seconds. Add ice and shake for an additional 5 seconds, then double-strain into a rocks glass over fresh ice. Raise the curtains and drink it up.

AS I LAY DRINKING

As I Lay Dying (1930)
by William Faulkner

Faulkner wrote his fifth novel in about as many weeks, and it reads like it—inspired and wild, and spit out by fifteen separate narrators in vexing, but thrilling, overlapping prose. In a simple-enough-sounding story that follows one family on its journey to bury their mother, Faulkner explores themes resonant with a post–World War II world, all rendered in his signature Southern style. Beat the heat with a party punch that ought to serve fifteen or so, depending on whom you invite.

SERVES 15 CHARACTERS
1 liter whiskey
3 ½ liters sweet tea
1 liter cranberry juice
1 liter lemon-lime soda

Combine all ingredients in a punch bowl and fill with ice. Ladle into mason jars over fresh ice. Say RIP to your thirst!

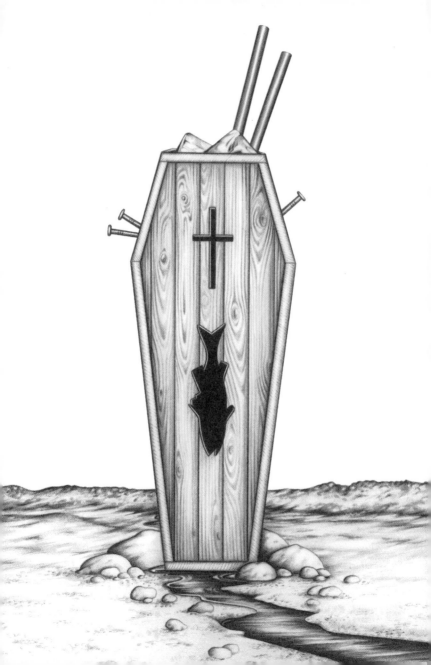

THE CALL OF
THE WILD TURKEY

The Call of the Wild (1903)

by Jack London

New rule: All protagonists should be dogs. In *The Call of the Wild*, our good boy Buck must answer the not-so-hypothetical question: If I were taken from my home in California and sold into slavery in the Yukon, would I rebel or give in—particularly since these fangs aren't doing much good in the suburbs? Though written over a hundred years ago, this *Call* still gets answered—in part because of Jack London's sharply observed signature theme of nature versus nurture. Drop a (Gold Rush–themed) Klondike bar (get it?) into this winter warmer that'll have you lying with dogs and toasting to your true nature.

> 2 ounces Wild Turkey bourbon
>
> 1 ounce Canadian Club whiskey
>
> 4 ounces hot water
>
> 2 ounces cinnamon syrup (page 14)
>
> 1 Klondike bar

Pour the bourbon, whiskey, water, and cinnamon syrup into a coffee mug. Drop in a Klondike bar to melt. Keep this one away from dogs.

ABSOLUT, ABSOLUT!

Absalom, Absalom! (1936)
by William Faulkner

Why tell a simple story if you can make it complicated? No worries—haters gonna hate (and Faulkner's gonna Faulkner). A truly exasperating exploration of life in the author's beloved, fictional Yoknapatawpha County, Mississippi, at least this story includes a "map" of the area. If out-of-order flashbacks and a Civil War backstory don't sound like your idea of a good time, keep in mind that Faulkner won no less than the Nobel, in part for his efforts here. This Southern sip is guaranteed to make you ramble incoherently.

½ ounce Absolut Vodka
½ ounce Absolut Citron
½ ounce Absolut Lime
½ ounce Absolut Vanilla
½ ounce Absolut Peach
5 ounces lemonade
Club soda, to fill
Lemon wheel and maraschino cherry, for garnish

Combine all the ingredients, except for the club soda and the garnishes, in a shaker with ice and shake for 5 seconds. Strain into a Collins glass over fresh ice and top with club soda. Garnish with a lemon wheel and a cherry, and just *try* to form a complete sentence.

DAVID COPPER MUG

David Copperfield (1849)
by Charles Dickens

No, not the magician who made the Statue of Liberty disappear back in the eighties. *David Copperfield* the *novel* began its life as a serialized story in a British newspaper (aka, author Charles Dickens's favorite way to roll out a story). In it, our poor title character grows up fatherless (and eventually motherless and brotherless), but ends up happily wedded—after suffering enough Dickensian troubles to make anyone reach for a drink. Our British-inspired mule should help the depressing parts go down fast.

2 ounces vodka
½ ounce lime juice
Ginger beer, to fill
½ ounce red wine, to float
Lime wheel, for garnish

Pour the vodka and lime juice into a copper mug. Fill with ice, add the ginger beer, and float the red wine on top. Garnish with a lime wheel and enjoy the dickens out of it.

PART II

CONTEMPORARY COCKTAILS

"In terms of emotional comfort it was our belief
that no amount of physical contact could match
the healing powers of a well-made cocktail."

—DAVID SEDARIS

It was queen of reading Oprah Winfrey who said, "Nothing can replace the experience of a good read" and king of comedy Groucho Marx who remarked, "Outside of a dog, a book is a man's best friend. Inside of a dog, it's too dark to read." Well-told tales are here to stay—and authors don't need to have a British accent for their work to be considered serious lit. This section of contemporary classics ranges from dystopia to erotica, united by the one thing that makes all stories more interesting—booze, baby.

THE HANDMAID'S ALE

The Handmaid's Tale (1985)
by Margaret Atwood

Marketed as a futuristic dystopian novel, Atwood's mid-eighties *Handmaid's Tale* was eerily prescient for any modern, thinking person who sees how women's bodies are still being regulated by men. Though it would take nearly thirty years for the book to be made into an Emmy-winning phenomenon, it never went out of print or off the shelves—perhaps because readers (and teachers) everywhere saw just how frustratingly resonant its themes remain. Take off your bonnet and drink up some justice.

> 4 ounces amber ale
> ½ ounce grain alcohol
> 2 ounces chamomile tea, cooled
> 1 ounce simple syrup (page 15)

Pour all ingredients into a Collins glass over ice and stir for 5 seconds. Drink him under the table (if not "under his eye").

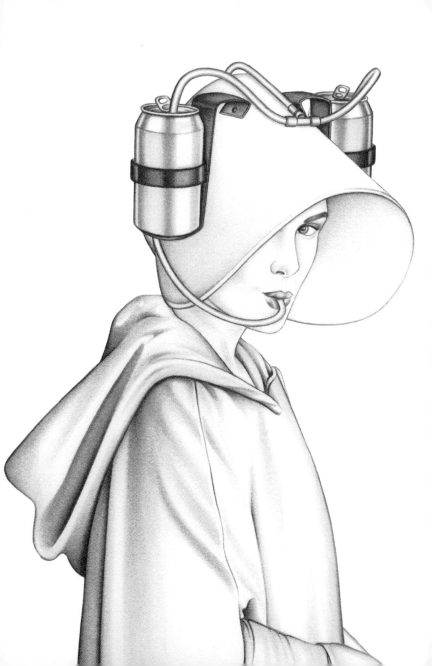

FIFTY SHADES
OF GREY GOOSE

Fifty Shades of Grey (2011)
by E. L. James

The kids are in bed. The husband's running late. It's mommy time. Though *Fifty Shades* started as *Twilight* fan fiction, it eventually whipped itself into shape to the tune of over 100 million copies sold, a $5 million movie deal, and a surprisingly sexy soundtrack. Snicker all you want—this smoldering saga of S&M gone naughtily right got America reading, flirting, and taking *very* long baths. Put away the handcuffs and pick up the shaker for a cocktail that'll get you goosed.

> 2 ounces Grey Goose vodka
> 2 ounces chocolate liqueur
> 2 ounces brewed lapsang souchong tea, cooled
> Whipped cream, for garnish
> Chocolate-covered strawberry, for garnish

Lock the bedroom door, light a candle, and pour the vodka, chocolate liqueur, and tea into a shaker with ice, and shake for 5 seconds. Strain into a coupe glass, top with whipped cream, and place a chocolate-covered strawberry on the rim.

EXTREMELY DRUNK AND INCREDIBLY CLOSE

Extremely Loud and Incredibly Close (2005)
by Jonathan Safran Foer

From the boy wonder who put the "it" in "literature," this follow-up to Foer's debut novel, *Everything Is Illuminated*, was among the first works of fiction post-9/11 to use the tragedy as a major plot point. In this case, we follow nine-year-old Oskar, whose father perishes in the Twin Towers, and who embarks on a New York City trek to find the missing lock that may or may not match up with a mysterious key. Critics were divided—but then, they hadn't tasted our twist on a classic Manhattan.

> 2 ½ ounces rye whiskey
> 1 ½ ounces sweet vermouth
> ½ ounce red wine

Pour the whiskey, sweet vermouth, and red wine into a mixing glass. Fill with ice and stir for 10 seconds. Strain into an "I ♥ NY" mug (or a rocks glass) and serve with a side of "big apple."

RABBIT, RUM

Rabbit, Run (1960)
by John Updike

Boy gets girl, boy gets girl pregnant, boy walks out in the end. Or rather, at the *beginning* of John Updike's seminal *Rabbit, Run*, where we meet a former basketball star who, at the ripe old age of twenty-six (hey, this was the late fifties!) decides his midlife crisis has arrived a bit early and goes hunting for greener pastures. (His nickname's Rabbit, after all.) The first in what would become a career-defining series that explored manhood in a changing America, Updike's book inspires a rum-based bevvie to get your tail twitching.

> 2 ounces spiced rum
>
> 2 ounces carrot juice
>
> 1 ounce lime juice
>
> 1 ounce simple syrup (page 15)
>
> Carrot-top greens, washed, for garnish

Pour all liquid ingredients into a shaker with ice and shake for 5 seconds. Strain into a coupe glass and garnish with the carrot-top greens. Hop to it!

THE HARD CIDER
HOUSE RULES

The Cider House Rules (1985)

by John Irving

Few contemporary novelists have been as widely read as John Irving—perhaps because few have had so many of their works adapted for the big screen. There was *The World According to Garp* (Robin Williams headlined that one), *Simon Birch* (based on *A Prayer for Owen Meany*), and *The Cider House Rules*—for which Irving himself won the Best Adapted Screenplay trophy at the 2000 Oscars. For this work, which is regularly compared to Dickens in its scope and subject matter, Irving explored the morality of human life from the point of view of a doctor and his protégé. Concoct a comforting hard cider for the orphans who figure prominently.

1 ounce whiskey

5 ounces hot apple cider

1 teaspoon Maine blueberry jam

1 cinnamon stick, for garnish

My mini-bar, my "rules"! Pour the first three ingredients into a coffee mug. Stir with a cinnamon stick and leave it in the mug as garnish.

A HEARTBREAKING WORK
OF STAGGERING GUINNESS

A Heartbreaking Work of Staggering Genius (2000)

by Dave Eggers

It takes guts to call a debut memoir "heartbreaking," let alone "genius," but then-unknown writer Dave Eggers lived up to the hype, and then some. This veritable doorstop opens with forty pages of "instructions" on how to read the book, and then goes on to chronicle Eggers's tragic misfortune of losing both his parents to cancer in the same year—before raising his much-younger brother by himself. A Pulitzer finalist that introduced the prolific Eggers to the world, a book this big deserves a drink this bold. Serve up a Gen X–worthy recipe that'll have you slurring your own sad story.

> 4 ounces Guinness
> 4 ounces eighties-era cola (like Crystal Pepsi)
> 2 ounces milk
> 1 ounce Nesquik chocolate syrup

Stream some classic eighties rock, pour all the ingredients into a Collins glass with ice, and stir. Prozac not required.

GO GET A SCOTCH, MAN

Go Set a Watchman (2015)

by Harper Lee

possibly too-good-to-be-true novel, *Go Set a Watchman* was published as Harper Lee's "follow-up" novel to *To Kill a Mockingbird*. The real-life story goes that a lawyer uncovered the unpublished manuscript in a safe deposit box, thrilled to discover the same characters (Scout! Atticus!) all grown up (and, in the latter's case, now spouting some arguably racist views). It proved an instant best seller *and* sparked quite a controversy, with some claiming the elderly Lee was being taken advantage of. Go get a scotch, man, and pull together some finely aged ingredients that are suspiciously delicious.

> 2 ounces scotch
>
> 2 ounces Campari
>
> 2 ounces sweet vermouth
>
> 3 dashes Angostura bitters

Pour all ingredients into a small Tupperware container. Let the mixture age until you forget about it (about 4 weeks), and then strain into a rocks glass over ice.

NINETEEN EIGHTY-FORTY

Nineteen Eighty-Four (1949)

by George Orwell

Written as a dire dystopian warning of the paranoid future world author George Orwell feared we'd descend to, *Nineteen Eighty-Four* shot up the best-seller lists once again during America's own recent political upheavals. With pioneering concepts such as Big Brother (the government is always watching) and propaganda standing in for news (see: your Facebook feed), it seems Orwell wasn't writing science fiction so much as realistic fiction that got there a few decades before the rest of us did. Draw the blinds and speak in a low whisper for forty ounces of pure '80s-flavor paranoia.

> 40 ounces malt liquor
>
> 2 ounces vodka
>
> 5 ounces liquid Tang
>
> 2 ounces orange juice

Combine all ingredients in a Thermos. Stop drinking when you feel like you're being watched. (And do *not* drink all 40 ounces in one or even five sittings.)

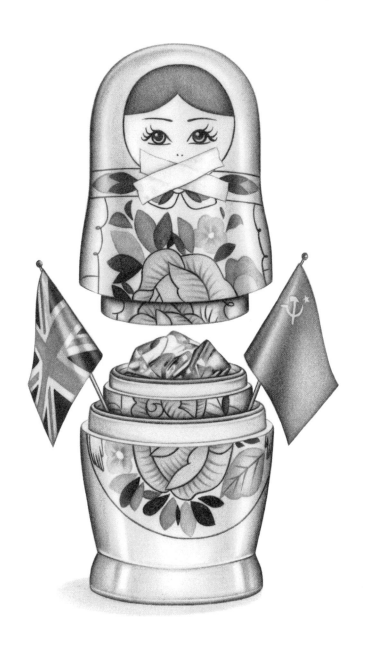

DRINKER TAILOR
SOLDIER SPY

Tinker Tailor Soldier Spy (1974)
by John le Carré

Move over, 007. A Soviet mole has infiltrated the uppermost ranks of the British Secret Service, and over-the-hill spy George Smiley is set to uncover the rat. Written by John le Carré, a former intelligence officer whose actual name is David John Moore Cornwell (how spylike to write under a fake name!), this book introduced dozens of spiffy spy terms, born wholly of le Carré's imagination. Sneak some booze on your next mission with a chilly Cold War cocktail worthy of a stakeout.

> 2 ounces vodka
> 3 ounces frozen cranberry juice concentrate
> 1 ounce cherry juice

Pour the vodka and juices into a rocks glass. Fill with ice and stir for 10 seconds. I spy an amazing drink!

THE DRINKING GAME OF THRONES

A Game of Thrones (1996)

by George R. R. Martin

Maybe it's the Tolkien-like setting, or the references to fur as lounge-wear, but George R. R. Martin's *Game of Thrones* universe seems to have been around forever—though the book only debuted in the mid-nineties. Martin has now killed off so many characters (and written so many pages) that he is said to rely upon his vast fandom to help keep all the subplots straight. This drink will have you seeing sideways—with a goblet full of fire and ice.

> 2 ounces scotch
> 1 ounce cinnamon whiskey (like Fireball)
> 1 ounce ginger liqueur
> 1 ounce lemon juice

Pour all ingredients into a shaker with ice and shake for 5 seconds. Strain into a goblet (or Collins glass) and settle into your throne.

GIN AND THE ART OF MOTORCYCLE MAINTENANCE

Zen and the Art of Motorcycle Maintenance (1974)

by Robert M. Pirsig

Author Robert M. Pirsig claims hundreds of publishers rejected his metaphysical faux autobiography before, of course, it sold millions of copies and helped bridge the gap between the psychedelic sixties and the excessive eighties. Ostensibly a road-trip tale shared by father and son, Pirsig asks deep philosophical questions about maintaining an Eastern mind-set in a Western world. Become one with your bar cart with our trippy gin-saki drink that'll be sure to rev up some engines.

> 1 ounce gin
>
> 1 ounce sake
>
> 1 ounce hemp milk
>
> 1 ounce Japanese yuzu juice (or grapefruit juice)
>
> 1 ounce simple syrup (page 15)

Pull that motorcycle over—I'm gonna need to see some ID. Pour all the ingredients into a shaker with ice and shake for 5 seconds. Strain into a coupe glass.

THE WINE OF BEAUTY

The Line of Beauty (2004)
by Alan Hollinghurst

We open in early-eighties England. Margaret Thatcher is in power, but our twenty-year-old protagonist is more concerned with being young and gay and just dipping a closeted toe into a world of carefree excess. He starts out inexperienced and wide-eyed before we jump to several years later, when he fully owns his homosexuality in a world now grappling with AIDS. Hollinghurst won the Man Booker Prize for a novel that serves as both a critical examination of the eighties and a celebration of its most precocious citizens. Blast some George Michael and serve up a witty wine cocktail that's fit for a Brit.

> 3 ounces white wine
> 2 ounces British gin (like Beefeater)
> 3 ounces brewed English breakfast tea, cooled
> 1 ounce vanilla syrup
> Edible flower, like hibiscus, to garnish

Pour all ingredients, except for the edible flower, into a shaker with ice and shake for 5 seconds. Strain into a tea cup (or mug) and garnish with an edible flower. Now, books down and pinkies up.

THE HITCHHIKER'S MUDSLIDE TO THE GALAXY

The Hitchhiker's Guide to the Galaxy (1979)

by Douglas Adams

With a Monty Python–esque sense of the absurd, Douglas Adams's *Hitchhiker* actually began its life as a BBC show before becoming an out-of-this-world-hilarious novel (not to mention a video game, a movie, comic book spin-offs, and countless parodies). As a road-trip comedy through the cosmos, starring the world's last living man, the universe of *Hitchhiker* titles contains nothing less than the answer to the meaning of life. Brace for impact with our Mars-worthy Mudslide that defies gravity.

> 1 ounce vodka
> 1 ounce Irish coffee liqueur (like Baileys)
> 1 ounce coffee liqueur (like Kahlúa)
> Heavy cream, to float
> Mars bar

Pour the vodka, Baileys, and Kahlúa into a rocks glass over ice. Slowly pour the cream on top. Chase it with a Mars bar—and brace for impact.

MUDDLESEX

Middlesex (2002)

by Jeffrey Eugenides

This decade-in-the-making follow-up to Eugenides's debut novel, *The Virgin Suicides*, found the author researching, writing, and rewriting the story of an intersex man and a member of three generations of Greek immigrants. Nearly uncategorizable in its scope and writing style, the novel started off slow in the sales department before the one-two combo of a Pulitzer Prize and Oprah's Book Club selection helped cement it as anything-but-middle-of-the-road. Serve up a sweet, sour, slightly ambiguous muddled Greek cocktail.

> 2 ounces gin
>
> ½ ounce ouzo
>
> 1 ounce lemon juice
>
> 1 ounce simple syrup (page 15)
>
> 5 fresh grapes, to muddle,
>   plus frozen grapes as garnish
>
> 2 figs, to muddle

Pour the gin, ouzo, lemon juice, and syrup into a shaker. Add the fresh grapes and figs and muddle them for 10 seconds. Add ice and shake for 10 seconds. Double-strain into a rocks glass over fresh ice. Garnish with frozen grapes—and prepare to Greek out.

THE BELLINI JAR

The Bell Jar (1963)
by Sylvia Plath

A dark and dizzyingly talented poet, Sylvia Plath struggled for years on this semiautobiographical novel before finally dashing off the complete text in seventy breathless days. A former magazine worker, Plath's severely depressed protagonist was a fictionalized version of herself. Plath's own mother requested that she publish the book under a pseudonym—which remained in place until years after Plath's death by suicide, when the world would finally learn her true identity. Serve up something sweeter than the fate that befell one of America's most talented, widely taught writers.

4 ounces prosecco

2 ounces elderflower liqueur (like St-Germain)

3 ounces peach puree (page 15)

1 peach slice, for garnish

Pour all ingredients, except for the peach slice, into a mason jar and stir. Garnish with a peach slice and think happy thoughts.

THE AMAZING ADVENTURES OF HAVE A BEER AND STAY

The Amazing Adventures of Kavalier and Clay (2000)
by Michael Chabon

This epic *kapow!* of a book somehow made sense of a Hitler-era world, as seen through the eyes of two comics-obsessed teenage boys, one of whom moonlights as a Houdini-esque escape artist. Michael Chabon won nearly every award with this lap-denter of a novel that leapt time periods in a single bound without so much as a hiccup. Speaking of hiccups: Settle in for a Prague-infused beer cocktail—and make two to share with a pal.

SERVES 2 ADVENTURERS

16 ounces pilsner beer

6 ounces apple juice

4 ounces lemon juice

Pour all ingredients into a small pitcher and stir. Divide evenly into two Collins glasses over ice. Serve with a side of schnitzel.

A TIME TO SWILL

A Time to Kill (1988)
by John Grisham

With a meager initial print run as a debut novel from an unknown lawyer, *A Time to Kill* wasn't exactly destined for hyperbolic success. (Until, that is, the film adaptation of the author's second book, *The Firm*, stirred up an appetite for the all-American legal thrillers that would cement John Grisham as a household name.) With echoes of *To Kill a Mockingbird*, Grisham's story of a young rape victim in a racially divided South was inspired by a similar story he overheard in the halls of his local courthouse. A time to kill? How about a time to *drink*. Take a seat on the porch and serve up this spiked sweet tea.

> 2 ounces tequila
> 1 ounce sweet vermouth
> 1 ounce Aperol
> 4 ounces sweet tea

Pour all the ingredients into a shaker with ice and shake for 5 seconds. Strain into a rocks glass over fresh ice and grab a gavel. Verdict: Guilty—of deliciousness!

ARE YOU THERE GOD?
IT'S ME, MARGARITA

Are You There God? It's Me, Margaret. (1970)
by Judy Blume

Back in the early seventies, Judy Blume became a living legend as a pioneering young adult novelist in the era before "young adult" even had a shelf at the bookstore. With *Margaret*, Blume wrote unflinchingly about weighty topics, ranging from religion to first kisses—prompting the book to be both banned across the land *and* embraced by generations of young women. (And men!) One classic deserves another, and our margarita recipe boasts a floral, "blume"-ing finish.

2 ounces tequila
¾ ounce lime juice
¾ ounce honey
½ ounce brewed hibiscus tea, cooled
Pinch of salt
1 sprig fresh lavender, for garnish

Uh, can we see some ID? Shake all ingredients, except for the lavender, in a shaker with ice for 5 seconds. Strain into a rocks glass over fresh ice and garnish with the lavender.

THE BLUEST MAI TAI

The Bluest Eye (1970)
by Toni Morrison

I n 1970 Toni Morrison was a successful editor of textbooks and a for-mer English teacher when, at nearly forty years old, she published this groundbreaking and unflinching novel, set in her native Ohio. Though she'd eventually go on to win nearly every important fiction prize there is, from the Nobel to the Pulitzer (with a Presidential Medal thrown in for good measure), Morrison's account of incest and racial identity was so true and unapologetic that it's still banned in some circles to this day. Shake your blues away with a drink as sweet and complex as Morrison's history-making prose.

2 ounces white rum

2 ounces dark rum

2 ounces orange juice

2 ounces blue pea flower (sold in the tea section)

1 ounce lime juice

1 ounce orgeat syrup

Orange wheel, for garnish

Pour all the liquid ingredients into a shaker with ice and shake for 5 seconds. Strain into a rocks glass over fresh ice. Garnish with an orange wheel, take a sip—and go change the world.

PART III

VIRGINAL VOLUMES

"Three be the things I shall never attain: Envy, content, and sufficient Champagne."

—DOROTHY PARKER

P ut down the booze and plug in a nightlight. This section features nonalcoholic (but thoroughly delicious) beverages inspired by history's most beloved bedtime tales (or tails, in the case of *Watership Down*). We've raided your childhood library for imbibe-worthy inspiration from moralistic bears, prairie-strong protagonists, and more frogs than you can shake a lily pad at. Who says you need a liquor license to throw a good book club?

THE WINE IN THE WILLOWS

The Wind in the Willows (1908)

by Kenneth Grahame

Here is a series of allegorical stories, starring talking animals in a quietly mystical Edwardian England. If *The Wind* reads like the perfect bedtime story, that's because it began its life as one. Author Kenneth Grahame, a retired banker, first got the idea for a blustering Toad and loyal Mole when putting his young sons to bed. What started with humble beginnings went on to be adapted into countless radio, TV, and stage performances—and even a wild ride at Disneyland. Serve up a faux-wine punch that sparkles like the author's posh prose.

> 3 ounces white grape juice
> (or spike it with 3 ounces white wine)
>
> 2 ounces grapefruit juice
>
> 2 ounces simple syrup (page 15)
>
> 4 basil sprigs, for garnish

Add the juices and simple syrup to a Collins glass filled with ice. Garnish with four basil sprigs. No animals were harmed in the making of this drink.

LORD OF THE PIMMS

Lord of the Rings (1954)
by J. R. R. Tolkien

An ingenious work of imagination, this new classic was written as if "translated" into English from one of J. R. R. Tolkien's fifteen made-up languages. With this work, the author was attempting a more ambitious literary quest than his earlier, easier-to-digest *Hobbit*. It took the author over a decade to construct his epic high fantasy, with an anxious publisher hoping it would live up to the promise of his earlier works. Spoiler alert: It did, and then some, eventually spawning a record-setting film franchise. Grab a goblet for a nonalcoholic Pimm's Cup that's worth a corner-store quest.

4 ounces lemon–lime soda (or 4 ounces Pimm's)

2 ounces grenadine (page 14)

1 ounce orange juice

1 ounce lemon juice

3 cucumber slices, for garnish

2 mint sprigs, for garnish

Pour all the liquid ingredients into a Collins glass. Garnish with cucumber and mint. If you like it, you'd better put a ring on it!

LONG ISLAND, THE WITCH, AND THE WARDROBE

The Lion, the Witch, and the Wardrobe (1950)

by C. S. Lewis

When author C. S. Lewis found himself housing child evacuees during World War II, he was struck by the possibility of writing for children; as a child himself, he'd had a vision of a faun holding an umbrella in a snowstorm, and at last he had an audience in mind to write it for. Early readers, including Lewis's contemporary, J. R. R. Tolkien, didn't quite "get" what Lewis was going for, causing the panged author to tear up the first draft. Nevertheless, he persisted—and the world was left with a series of enchanting (and allegorically Christian) books that still set the standard for fantasy with heart. Toast to a perpetual winter with a frozen iced tea you'll guard like a lion.

> 4 ounces iced tea
> (or 4 ounces hard iced tea, like Twisted Tea)
>
> 3 ounces cola
>
> 2 ounces simple syrup (page 15)
>
> 1 ounce lemon juice

Place all ingredients in a container and let sit in a freezer for 4 hours. Take out of the freezer and place into a blender with a few ice cubes. Blend for 7 seconds and pour into a pint glass. Garnish with a cocktail umbrella.

WATERSHIP DOWN
THE HATCH

Watership Down (1972)
by Richard Adams

Initially rejected as both too kiddy for older readers and too scary for little ones, once *Watership* was published it became an instant, unlikely hit—and is still going home in backpacks today. Starring a group of English rabbits, one of whom has a bunny version of ESP (okay, sure), the novel began its life, as so many children's classics seem to, as a series of improvised stories the author told his daughters on drives through the English countryside. You'll hop for our carrot juice "cocktail" that'll get lips *and* noses twitching.

> 4 ounces carrot juice
> 2 ounces lime juice
> 1 ounce honey
> Club soda, to fill
> 2 mint sprigs, for garnish

A little something for every-bunny: Pour the carrot juice, lime juice, and honey into a Collins glass over ice. Top with club soda and garnish with mint sprigs.

LITTLE SOUSED
ON THE PRAIRIE

Little House on the Prairie (1935)
by Laura Ingalls Wilder

Perhaps best known to a generation as a gentle TV show, *Little House* began as a series of autobiographical novels about Laura Ingalls Wilder's life as a young pioneer in the late-1880s Midwest. With achingly earnest prose that covered everything from brutal winters to bear attacks, Ingalls Wilder launched a franchise that included not just the TV show but a stage adaptation starring little "Laura," Melissa Gilbert, as the now-grown-up "Ma." Serve up a "half pint" of prairie-fresh ingredients for your own little pioneers.

Stay sober: 4 ounces sweet tea (or get soused: 4 ounces hard iced tea, like Twisted Tea)

3 ounces lemonade

1 peach slice, for garnish

Toss your corn husk doll aside and pour all ingredients, except for the peach, into a mason jar over ice. Garnish with a peach slice.

FROG AND TOAD
ARE SOBER

Frog and Toad Are Friends (1970)
by Arnold Lobel

When author Arnold Lobel was a child, he spent much of his second-grade year bedridden at home. Upon his return to school, he counted among his friends a series of drawings and characters he'd created while sick, in part to combat his social anxiety. After growing up and writing the stories in earnest, Lobel's enduring *Frog and Toad* stories are said to be manifestations of different parts of his personality, and the books' folksy morality and cross-species friendship earned the series Caldecott and Newbery honors. Ribbit? How about *drink* it!

> 2 ounces lemon juice
>
> 1 ounce lime juice
>
> 2 ounces simple syrup (page 15)
>
> Basil, for muddling, plus 1 leaf for garnish
>
> Cucumber-infused ice cubes (dice a cucumber
>   and add it with water to an ice cube tray)

Place the juices, simple syrup, and basil in a shaker and muddle for 10 seconds. Fill with ice and shake for 5 seconds. Strain into a Collins glass filled with cucumber-infused ice. Garnish with a floating "lily pad" basil leaf on top.

GOODNIGHT MOONSHINE

Goodnight Moon (1947)

by Margaret Wise Brown

While it's hard to imagine anything as tender as *Goodnight Moon* being groundbreaking, at the time of its publication nearly all children's books focused on fairy tales or moralistic stories. Margaret Wise Brown, who had studied early childhood development, had a hunch that young children would enjoy a close look at the everyday objects that made up their little lives—though not everyone understood what the author was going for, at first. With millions of books sold and even more bedtimes hastened, Wise Brown gets the last laugh—and yawn. You will, too, with a sleepy-time drink that'll send you jumping (or snoring) over the moon.

> 4 ounces brewed chamomile tea
> 3 ounces warm milk
> 1 ounce honey

Place all ingredients in a mug and stir with a spoon. Serve with a Moonpie. (For a spiked moonshine version, add 2 ounces of whiskey, warmed for 20 seconds in the microwave.)

CAPS FOR ALE

Caps for Sale (1940)
by Esphyr Slobodkina

A classic read-aloud and a natural counting book, owing to its teetering stack of hipster-style caps, this book was reportedly based on a folktale before Russian author (and noted feminist) Slobodkina made it her own. This tale of a napping salesman and the monkeys who stir up trouble when they steal his hats still delights children, and for good reason—this abstract artist (and frequent collaborator of Margaret Wise Brown) had an innate feel for the absurd. You'll go bananas for our faux ale cocktail.

> 3 ounces ginger ale
> 2 ounces pineapple juice
> Chopped frozen banana, as "ice"
> Banana chips, for garnish

Quit monkeying around. Place the ginger ale and pineapple juice in a Collins glass over the banana "ice cubes." Garnish with the banana chips.

THE BERENSTAIN BEERS

The Berenstain Bears (1962)
by Stan and Jan Berenstain

First off, let's get one thing straight: It's not the Beren*steen* Bears, it's Berenstain, with an "a." Many of us grew up in a house littered with (and a mind enlightened by) this sprawling series, which covered such timeworn topics as Trouble with Money, Trouble with Chores, and Trouble with Neighbors. Okay, that last one was actually called *The New Neighbors*, and it featured an oddly bigoted Papa Bear annoyed with the brand-new pandas who had just moved in across the lawn. (With hundreds of titles, they can't all be winners.) Pitch a tent for a honey "beer" that'll have you pawing at the cupboard for more.

> 4 ounces hot water
> 2 ounces ginger beer
> 1 ounce honey
> 2 cinnamon sticks

Combine all ingredients in a coffee mug and stir. Prepare to hibernate for the night.

THE SEAGRAM'S GARDEN

The Secret Garden (1911)

by Frances Hodgson Burnett

Proving that even the brattiest among us seem to lighten up once we get a little nature under our nails, *The Secret Garden* finds newly orphaned Mary Lennox picking up her roots (sorry) to go live with a withdrawn uncle in a faraway corner of England. Lucky for Mary, same-age playmates await, as does an enchanted and seemingly dead garden that needs her touch to make its greenery grow again. Put down the hoe and pick up a highball for green-thumb ingredients with a mock-whiskey finish.

> 5 ounces Seagram's ginger ale
> 2 ounces watermelon juice
> 1 mint sprig, for garnish

Pour the ginger ale and juice into a highball glass over ice. Garnish with a mint sprig. Now get outside and play. (For a spiked version, use 2 ounces of whiskey, like Seagram's 7, and 3 ounces of ginger ale instead of 5.)

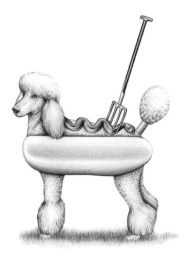

PART IV

SCHOLARLY SNACKS

> "I hate people who are not serious about meals. It is so shallow of them."
>
> —OSCAR WILDE

Never read on an empty stomach. Some books are so dense and delicious, they call out for something more substantial than a mere sip can provide. (Hey, *War and Peace,* are your ears burning?) Enter: The snack bar—because nothing's more appetizing than a story well told. Don't worry about getting crumbs in bed (or on the pages, for that matter). We'd eat these delectable tomes, too, if we could. From salads to sweets, we've got your hunger covered—and your next great read selected. *Book appétit!*

ANIMAL CRACKERS FARM

Animal Farm (1945)

by George Orwell

*C*harlotte's Web it ain't. Orwell made no bones about his intention with this novel: to fuse his anti-Stalinist political views with a satirical-cum-allegorical tale of scheming pigs intent on leading a revolt against the farmers. Initially rejected by many publishers (Imagine *that* pitch meeting: "It's an anticommunist tale set among a frustrated faction of . . . literal hogs—and kids will love it!"), the book would become a classic of the genre and required reading for nearly all American kids. You'll pig out on our homemade animal crackers.

MAKES ABOUT 35 COOKIES

2 ½ cups all-purpose flour

1 teaspoon baking powder

1 teaspoon salt

¼ teaspoon grated nutmeg

12 tablespoons (1 ½ sticks) salted butter

1 cup granulated sugar

2 eggs

1 teaspoon vanilla extract

Sift together the flour, baking powder, salt, and nutmeg in a medium bowl. In a large bowl, beat the butter with an electric mixer for 1 minute, then add the sugar, eggs, and vanilla and beat until mixed. Slowly add the flour mixture and beat for about 2 minutes, or until all ingredients are combined.

Divide the dough in half, shape each half into a ball, wrap the two halves in plastic wrap, and place them in the fridge for 1 hour, at least, and preferably overnight.

When you're ready to make the cookies, preheat the oven to 350°F. Unwrap each dough ball and roll them into thin disks, approximately ¼ inch thick, on a floured surface. Using animal cookie shapes (extra points for barn-yard animals), cut out your animals and place them on a baking sheet. Bake for 15 minutes, or until golden, and transfer to a cooling rack. It's feedin' time!

SALADS FOR ALGERNON

Flowers for Algernon (1966)
by Daniel Keyes

Originally a short story before its expansion into a novel (and eventually the Oscar-winning film *Charly*), these flowers nearly didn't sprout; publishers found the realistic portrayal of the mentally disabled to be too much of a downer for readers, and encouraged author Daniel Keyes to give a Hollywood ending to his account of a mentally ill adult who goes under the knife for an experimental IQ-enhancing surgery. Keyes insisted on a more tragic (read: believable) ending, and the work became a classic. Break out our edible bouquet that's bound to brighten any day.

SERVES 2

Dressing
½ tablespoon whole grain mustard

1 shallot, peeled and diced

2 ounces red wine vinegar

2 ounces extra virgin olive oil

Greens
5 ounces leafy greens (like romaine lettuce), washed

1 handful edible flower petals (like hibiscus)

Combine the mustard, shallot, and vinegar in a large bowl and slowly mix in the olive oil. Add the greens and flowers, and toss just before serving. Talk about bloomin' delicious!

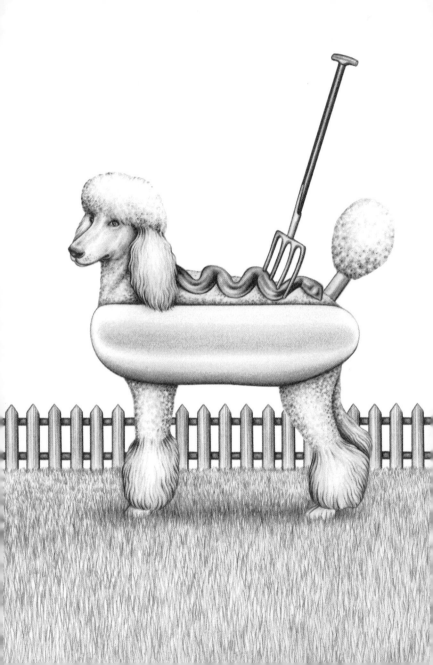

THE CURIOUS INCIDENT
OF THE HOT DOG
IN THE NIGHTTIME

The Curious Incident of the Dog in the Nighttime (2003)
by Mark Haddon

The first book to simultaneously be published with two different covers (one for teens, one for adults), this curious novel enchanted readers worldwide, no matter what their age. A coming-of-age mystery that quotes Sherlock Holmes for its title, Haddon's story of a young savant accused of murdering a neighbor's poodle is a tour-de-force journey across London. A polarizing but popular title that found brilliant life in a stage adaptation, this masterwork inspires a midnight-snack hot dog dish that'll set tails and tongues wagging.

MAKES 24 MINI HOT DOGS

1 (8-ounce) can crescent roll dough

24 cocktail weenies

British "brown sauce," as a condiment
(like HP Sauce)

Preheat your oven to 350°F. Pop open the can of dough and unroll into 8 large triangles of dough. Slice each triangle into 3 smaller triangular parts, leaving 24 slices of dough. Roll each cocktail weenie up in a slice of dough, place on a baking sheet, and bake for approximately 15 minutes, or until golden. Serve with British "brown sauce." No doggie bag required.

THE FRIDGES OF
MADISON COUNTY

The Bridges of Madison County (1992)
by Robert James Waller

A lonely Italian war bride in Madison County, Iowa, gets an unexpected lift when a visiting photographer shows up to take photos of her town's bridges. (So *that's* what the kids are calling it these days.) It was a simple enough premise that made for a slim enough novella—albeit one that went on to sell over sixty million copies, topped the bestseller lists for a record number of weeks, and got the Clint Eastwood–Meryl Streep adaptation treatment, and all despite snickers that the source material was an overwrought story of lust at first sight. Cool off your own indiscretions with Iowa's favorite pie—pulled straight from the fridge—to help rebuild your own bridges.

> ¼ cup cornstarch
> ¾ cup tap water, divided
> Juice from ½ lemon, about 1 ounce
> 1 cup granulated sugar
> 2 cups chopped rhubarb
> 2 cups chopped strawberries
> 2 tablespoons salted butter
> 1 teaspoon vanilla extract
> 1 (9-inch) prebaked pie crust
> Whipped cream or ice cream, for garnish

Combine the cornstarch, ¼ cup of water, and lemon juice in a small bowl, and mix until combined. In a small saucepan over medium-high heat, combine the sugar, rhubarb, and remaining water. Heat to a boil, reduce to medium heat, and simmer for 5 minutes. Add the cornstarch mixture and stir for 2 minutes.

Remove from heat and stir in the strawberries, butter, and vanilla. Pour the mixture into the crust and refrigerate for 2 to 4 hours, or until firm. Garnish with whipped cream or ice cream—and don't forget to take a picture.

WAR AND PEAS

War and Peace (1869)
by Leo Tolstoy

Think *War and Peace* is tough to read? Try writing it! Tolstoy reportedly developed migraines during his six-year battle with the page, though he eventually grew so impressed with his own work, he insisted it was too uncategorizable to be called a novel. This Russian epic is not only a sweeping family saga, but also a veritable history of how wars were actually won (and lost), owing to Tolstoy's commitment to scouting out battlefields for in-the-field accuracy. You'll fight like hell for our Russian split pea soup to power you through the next long winter.

SERVES BETWEEN 6 AND 8

1 cup Russian vodka
1 pound dried peas, rinsed
7 cups water
1 onion, chopped
1 large celery stalk, chopped
Salt and pepper, to taste
2 large carrots, chopped

Place the vodka, peas, and water in a large pot over high heat and bring to a boil. Reduce to medium-high heat, add the onion and celery, and salt and pepper to taste, and simmer for about an hour. Add the carrots and simmer for an additional 15 minutes. Let cool slightly before serving. Google "how to say *bon appétit* in Russian," and go to town.

BANANA KARENINA

Anna Karenina (1877)

by Leo Tolstoy

This is the novel that *other* novelists, from Faulkner to Tolstoy's fellow Russians Dostoyevsky and Nabokov, call the best novel ever. An eight-part epic with a family tree so vast it's practically a forest, this book's author wrote its tragic love affair over many installments before compiling the entire volume into one back-and-heart-breaking tome. Tolstoy being Tolstoy, he wasn't content to write a simple rom-com, instead setting the entire thing against the political landscape of a complicated nineteenth-century Russia. Enjoy a White Russian banana split that's Siberian-cold and love-affair hot.

> 1 banana, peeled
> 2 scoops vanilla ice cream
> 1 dollop whipped cream
> Kahlúa, to drizzle
> 2 cherries, presoaked in vodka

Slice the banana in half, place the two halves in a bowl, and place all ingredients on top. Best dessert ever? Hard to say, but it's def epic.

Drinking Game

Faulkner goes off plot.

Tolstoy casually introduces another character in the six-hundred-person-strong *War and Peace*.

You accidentally refer to Frankenstein as the monster, not the *doctor*.

James Patterson publishes another book.

The book was better than the movie.

You use Wikipedia to write a term paper in lieu of actually reading the book. (*Take two shots* if your teacher didn't catch you.) (*Take three shots* if you got an A.)

You actually read *Playboy*
just for the articles.

Someone asks what you're planning
to do with a BA in English.

You increased the font size on a paper in order to
make the required page count.

Formulas for Metric Conversion

Ounces to grams..........multiply ounces by 28.35
Pounds to grams..........multiply pounds by 453.5
Cups to liters..........multiply cups by .24
Fahrenheit to Centigrade..........subtract 32 from Fahrenheit,
   multiply by 5 and divide by 9

METRIC EQUIVALENTS FOR VOLUME

U.S.	Metric
⅛ tsp.	0.6 ml
¼ tsp.	1.2 ml
½ tsp.	2.5 ml
¾ tsp.	3.7 ml
1 tsp.	5 ml
1½ tsp.	7.4 ml
2 tsp.	10 ml
1 Tbsp.	15 ml
1½ Tbsp.	22.0 ml
2 Tbsp. (⅛ cup/1 fl. oz)	30 ml
3 Tbsp.	45 ml
¼ cup (2 fl. oz)	59 ml
⅓ cup	79 ml
½ cup (4 fl. oz)	118 ml
⅔ cup	158 ml
¾ cup (6 fl. oz)	178 ml
1 cup (8 fl. oz)	237 ml
1¼ cups	300 ml
1½ cups	355 ml
1¾ cups	425 ml
2 cups (1 pint/16 fl. oz)	500 ml
3 cups	725 ml
4 cups (1 quart/32 fl. oz)	.95 liters
16 cups (1 gallon/128 fl. oz)	3.8 liters

OVEN TEMPERATURES

Degrees Fahrenheit	Degrees Centigrade	British Gas Marks
200°	93°	—
250°	120°	½
275°	140°	1
300°	150°	2
325°	165°	3
350°	175°	4
375°	190°	5
400°	200°	6
450°	230°	8

METRIC EQUIVALENTS FOR WEIGHT

U.S.	Metric
1 oz	28 g
2 oz	57 g
3 oz	85 g
4 oz	113 g
5 oz	142 g
6 oz	170 g
7 oz	198 g
8 oz	227 g
16 oz (1 lb.)	454 g
2.2 lbs.	1 kilogram

METRIC EQUIVALENTS FOR BUTTER

U.S.	Metric
2 tsp.	10 g
1 Tbsp.	15 g
1½ Tbsp.	22.5 g
2 Tbsp. (1 oz)	27 g
3 Tbsp.	42 g
4 Tbsp.	56 g
4 oz. (1 stick)	110 g
8 oz. (2 sticks)	220 g

METRIC EQUIVALENTS FOR LENGTH

U.S.	Metric
¼ inch	.65 cm
½ inch	1.25 cm
1 inch	2.50 cm
2 inches	5.00 cm
3 inches	6.00 cm
4 inches	8.00 cm
5 inches	11.00 cm
6 inches	15.00 cm
7 inches	18.00 cm
8 inches	20.00 cm
9 inches	23.00 cm
12 inches	30.50 cm
15 inches	38.00 cm

ACKNOWLEDGMENTS

A grateful, slightly tipsy thanks to: the entire staff at Running Press and Hachette, especially my editor, Jordana Tusman, along with Kristin Kiser, Susan Weinberg, Seta Zink, Jessica Schmidt, Jennifer Kasius, Geri DiTella, and Cassie Drumm; copy editor Diana Drew; proofreader Katie Wilson; book designer Josh McDonnell; illustrator Lauren Mortimer; my writer guardian angel, Cheri Steinkellner; my agent, Brenda Bowen; my boyfriend, David; my research assistant, Ashley Latimer; my Airbnb hosts Adam and RB in Hudson, New York, where I wrote/drank through much of the manuscript; and Cody Goldstein, whose cocktail expertise is always invaluable and delicious.

Thank you, especially, to the authors cited, whose works inspire my own. (Especially writers who choose really long titles, which are easier to make puns from.) Your books deserve three cheers and you deserve unlimited cocktails. Particularly you, Ms. Judy Blume!

Lastly but mostly, thank you to my readers, especially those who tag #TequilaMockingbird on Instagram. Because the only thing more fun than writing these books is spying on people enjoying them.

INDEX

A

Absalom, Absalom! (Faulkner), 54

Absolut, Absolut!, 54

Adams, Douglas, *The Hitchhiker's Guide to the Galaxy,* 81

Adams, Richard, *Watership Down,* 101

The Amazing Adventures of Have a Beer and Stay, 87

The Amazing Adventures of Kavalier and Clay (Chabon), 87

Angostura bitters, 13

   Go Get a Scotch, Man, 69

   Madame Brewery, 39

Animal Crackers Farm, 113–14

Animal Farm (Orwell), 113

Anna Karenina (Tolstoy), 122

Aperol

   Tender is the Nightcap, 18

   A Time to Swill, 88

apple cider, apple juice

   The Amazing Adventures of Have a Beer and Stay, 87

   The Hard Cider House Rules, 66

Are You There God? It's Me, Margaret (Blume), 90

Are You There God? It's Me, Margarita, 90

As I Lay Drinking, 50

As I Lay Dying (Faulkner), 50

Atwood, Margaret, *The Handmaid's Tale,* 58

B

Baileys, *in* Portrait of the Artist as a Drunk Man, 20

bananas

   Banana Karenina, 122

   Caps for Ale, 106

beer, 12

   The Amazing Adventures of Have a Beer and Stay, 87

   Billy Budd Light, 33

   The Canterbury Ales, 36

   The Handmaid's Ale, 58

   A Heartbreaking Work of Staggering Guinness, 68

   Madame Brewery, 39

   Nineteen Eighty-Forty, 70

The Bellini Jar, 84

The Bell Jar (Plath), 84

Berenstain, Stan and Jan, *The Berenstain Bears,* 109

The Berenstain Beers, 107

Billy Budd Light, 33

Billy Budd (Melville), 33

blueberries, blueberry jam

   The Hard Cider House Rules, 66

   Of Mice and Manischewitz, 41

blue curaçao, *in* A Room with Vermouth, 49

The Bluest Eye (Morrison), 91

The Bluest Mai Tai, 91

Blume, Judy, *Are You There God? It's Me, Margaret,* 90

bourbon

The Call of the Wild Turkey, 53

Lord Jim Beam, 42

The Bridges of Madison County (Waller), 118

The Brothers Kamikaze, 47

The Brothers Karamazov (Dostoyevsky), 47

Brown, Margaret Wise, *Goodnight Moon,* 104

Burnett, Frances Hodgson, *The Secret Garden,* 108

C

The Call of the Wild (London), 53

The Call of the Wild Turkey, 53

Campari, *in* Go Get a Scotch, Man, 69

Canadian Club whiskey, *in* The Call of the Wild Turkey, 53

The Canterbury Ales, 36

The Canterbury Tales (Chaucer), 36

Caps for Ale, 108

Caps for Sale (Slobodkina), 106

carrot juice

Rabbit, Rum, 65

Watership Down the Hatch, 101

Chabon, Michael, *The Amazing Adventures of Kavalier and Clay,* 87

Champagne

Dangerous Libations, 44

She Stoops to Cointreau, 26

Chaucer, Geoffrey, *The Canterbury Tales,* 36

chocolate, chocolate liqueur

The Canterbury Ales, 36

Fifty Shades of Grey Goose, 60

A Heartbreaking Work of Staggering Guinness, 68

Murder on the Orient Espresso, 29

Christie, Agatha, *Murder on the Orient Express,* 29

The Cider House Rules (Irving), 66

cinnamon syrup: to make, 14

Lord Jim Beam, 42

clamato, *in* Billy Budd Light, 33

coffee, coffee liqueur

The Hitchhiker's Mudslide to the Galaxy, 81

Madame Brewery, 39

Murder on the Orient Espresso, 29

Cointreau

The Brothers Kamikaze, 47

She Stoops to Cointreau, 26

Conrad, Joseph, *Lord Jim,* 42

cranberry juice

Drinker Tailor Soldier Spy, 73

As I Lay Drinking, 50

crème de cassis, *in* Dangerous Libations, 44

The Curious Incident of the Dog in the Nighttime (Haddon), 117

The Curious Incident of the Hot Dog in the Nighttime, 117

D

Dangerous Liaisons (Laclos), 44

Dangerous Libations, 44

David Copperfield (Dickens), 55

David Copper Mug, 55

Dickens, Charles, *David Copperfield,* 55

Dostoyevsky, Fyodor, *The Brothers Karamazov,* 47

Doyle, Sir Arthur Conan, *The Hound of the Baskervilles,* 30

Drinker Tailor Soldier Spy, 73

drinking game, 123–24

The Drinking Game of Thrones, 75

E

Eggers, Dave, *A Heartbreaking Work of Staggering Genius,* 68

elderflower liqueur, *in* The Bellini Jar, 84

Eugenides, Jeffrey, *(Middlesex),* 82

Extremely Drunk and Incredibly Close, 63

Extremely Loud and Incredibly Close (Foer), 63

F

Faulkner, William
  Absalom, Absalom!, 54
  As I Lay Dying, 50

Fifty Shades of Grey Goose, 60

Fifty Shades of Grey (James), 60

Fitzgerald, F. Scott, *Tender is the Night,* 18

Flaubert, Gustave, *Madame Bovary,* 39

flavorings, 13–15

Flowers for Algernon (Keyes), 115

Foer, Jonathan Safran, *Extremely Loud and Incredibly Close,* 63

Forster, E. M., *A Room with a View,* 49

The Fridges of Madison County, 118–20

Frog and Toad Are Friends (Lobel), 103

Frog and Toad Are Sober, 103

G

A Game of Thrones (Martin), 75

garnishing techniques, 9

gin, 10
  Gin and the Art of Motorcycle Maintenance, 76
  The Greyhound of the Baskervilles, 30
  Muddlesex, 82
  The Wine of Beauty, 79

ginger ale, ginger beer, ginger liqueur
  The Berenstain Beers, 107
  Caps for Ale, 106
  David Copper Mug, 55
  The Drinking Game of Thrones, 75
  The Seagram's Garden, 108

glassware, 3–4

Go Get a Scotch, Man, 69

Goldsmith, Oliver, *She Stoops to Conquer,* 26

Goodnight Moon (Brown), 104

Goodnight Moonshine, 104

Go Set a Watchman (Lee), 69

Grahame, Kenneth, *The Wind in the Willows,* 95

grapefruit juice
  The Brothers Kamikaze, 47
  Gin and the Art of Motorcycle Maintenance, 76
  The Greyhound of the Baskervilles, 30
  The Wine in the Willows, 95

grape juice
  The Grappa of Wrath, 25
  The Wine in the Willows, 97

The Grapes of Wrath (Steinbeck), 25

The Grappa of Wrath, 25

grenadine syrup: to make, 14

Lord of the Pimms, 96

The Tequila Sun Also Rises, 35

Grey Goose vodka, *in* Fifty Shades of Grey Goose, 60

The Greyhound of the Baskervilles, 30

Grisham, John, *A Time to Kill,* 88

Guinness, *in* A Heartbreaking Work of Staggering Guinness, 68

H

Haddon, Mark, *The Curious Incident of the Dog in the Nighttime,* 117

The Handmaid's Ale, 58

The Handmaid's Tale (Atwood), 58

The Hard Cider House Rules, 66

hazelnut liqueur

The Canterbury Ales, 36

Portrait of the Artist as a Drunk Man, 20

A Heartbreaking Work of Staggering Genius (Eggers), 68

A Heartbreaking Work of Staggering Guinness, 68

Hemingway, Ernest, *The Sun Also Rises,* 35

The Hitchhiker's Guide to the Galaxy (Adams), 81

The Hitchhiker's Mudslide to the Galaxy, 81

Hollinghurst, Alan, *The Line of Beauty,* 79

The Hound of the Baskervilles (Doyle), 30

I

Irving, John, *The Cider House Rules,* 66

The Island of Dr. Merlot, 23

The Island of Dr. Moreau (Wells), 23

J

James, E. L., *Fifty Shades of Grey,* 60

Jim Beam bourbon, *in* Lord Jim Beam, 42

Joyce, James, *Portrait of the Artist as a Young Man,* 20

K

Keyes, Daniel, *Flowers for Algernon,* 115

L

Laclos, Pierre Choderlos de, *Dangerous Liaisons,* 44

Le Carré, John, *Tinker Tailor Soldier Spy,* 73

Lee, Harper, *Go Set a Watchman,* 69

lemonade, lemon-lime soda

Absolut, Absolut!, 54

As I Lay Drinking, 50

Little Soused on the Prairie, 102

Lord of the Pimms, 96

Lewis, C. S., *The Lion, the Witch, and the Wardrobe,* 101

The Line of Beauty (Hollinghurst), 81

The Lion, the Witch, and the Wardrobe (Lewis), 99

liqueurs, about, 11. *See also specific liqueurs*

Little House on the Prairie (Wilder), 102

Little Soused on the Prairie, 102

Lobel, Arnold, *Frog and Toad Are Friends,* 103

London, Jack, *The Call of the Wild,* 53

Long Island, the Witch, and the Wardrobe, 99

Lord Jim Beam, 42

Lord Jim (Conrad), 42

Lord of the Pimms, 96

Lord of the Rings (Tolkien), 96

M

Madame Bovary (Flaubert), 39

Madame Brewery, 39

Manischewitz red wine, *in* Of Mice and Manischewitz, 41

Martin, George R. R., *A Game of Thrones,* 75

measurement conversions, 125

Melville, Herman, *Billy Budd,* 33

Merlot, *in* The Island of Dr. Merlot, 23

Middlesex (Eugenides), 82

milk

Gin and the Art of Motorcycle Maintenance, 76

Goodnight Moonshine, 104

A Heartbreaking Work of Staggering Guinness, 68

Morrison, Toni, *The Bluest Eye,* 91

Muddlesex, 82

Murder on the Orient Espresso, 29

Murder on the Orient Express (Christie), 29

N

Nineteen Eighty-Forty, 70

Nineteen Eighty-Four (Orwell), 70

nonalcoholic drinks

The Berenstain Beers, 107

Caps for Ale, 106

Frog and Toad Are Sober, 103

Goodnight Moonshine, 104

Little Soused on the Prairie, 102

Long Island, the Witch, and the Wardrobe, 99

Lord of the Pimms, 96

The Seagram's Garden, 108

Watership Down the Hatch, 101

The Wine in the Willows, 95

O

Of Mice and Manischewitz, 41

Of Mice and Men (Steinbeck), 41

orange juice

The Bluest Mai Tai, 91

The Brothers Kamikaze, 47

The Island of Dr. Merlot, 23

Lord of the Pimms, 96

Nineteen Eighty-Forty, 70

The Tequila Sun Also Rises, 35

orgeat syrup, 15

The Bluest Mai Tai, 91

Lord Jim Beam, 42

Orwell, George

Animal Farm, 113

Nineteen Eighty-Four, 70

ouzo, *in* Muddlesex, 82

P

pastis, *in* Madame Brewery, 39

peach puree: to make, 15

The Bellini Jar, 84

Pimm's, *in* Lord of the Pimms, 96

pineapple juice

Caps for Ale, 106

The Island of Dr. Merlot, 23

Lord Jim Beam, 42

Pirsig, Robert M., *Zen and the Art of Motorcycle Maintenance,* 76

Plath, Sylvia, *The Bell Jar,* 84

Portrait of the Artist as a Drunk Man, 20

Portrait of the Artist as a Young Man (Joyce), 20

prosecco

The Bellini Jar, 84

Tender is the Nightcap, 18

R

Rabbit, Rum, 65

Rabbit, Run (Updike), 65

A Room with a View (Forster), 49

A Room with Vermouth, 49

rum, 10

The Bluest Mai Tai, 91

Rabbit, Rum, 65

rye whiskey, *in* Extremely Drunk and Incredibly Close, 63

S

sake, *in* Gin and the Art of Motorcycle Maintenance, 76

Salads for Algernon, 115

scotch

The Drinking Game of Thrones, 75

Go Get a Scotch, Man, 69

The Seagram's Garden, 108

The Secret Garden (Burnett), 108

She Stoops to Cointreau, 26

She Stoops to Conquer (Goldsmith), 26

simple syrup, to make, 15

Slobodkina, Esphyr, *Caps for Sale,* 106

snacks

Animal Crackers Farm, 113–14

Banana Karenina, 122

The Curious Incident of the Hot Dog in the Nighttime, 117

The Fridges of Madison County, 118–20

Salads for Algernon, 115

War and Peas, 121

sour mix, to make, 15

Steinbeck, John

The Grapes of Wrath, 25

Of Mice and Men, 41

The Sun Also Rises (Hemingway), 35

T

tea

Are You There God? It's Me, Margarita, 90

Fifty Shades of Grey Goose, 60

Goodnight Moonshine, 104

The Handmaid's Ale, 58

As I Lay Drinking, 50

Little Soused on the Prairie, 102

Long Island, the Witch, and the Wardrobe, 99

A Time to Swill, 88

The Wine of Beauty, 79

techniques for making and decorating drinks, 7–9

Tender is the Nightcap, 18

Tender is the Night (Fitzgerald), 18

tequila, 10

  Are You There God? It's Me, Margarita, 90

  The Tequila Sun Also Rises, 35

  A Time to Swill, 88

terminology, 10–15

A Time to Kill (Grisham), 88

A Time to Swill, 88

Tinker Tailor Soldier Spy (le Carré), 73

Tolkien, J. R. R., *Lord of the Rings,* 96

Tolstoy, Leo

  Anna Karenina, 122

  War and Peace, 121

tools and equipment, 3–6

triple sec, *in* The Brothers Kamikaze, 47

U

Updike, John, *Rabbit, Run,* 65

V

vermouth

  Extremely Drunk and Incredibly Close, 63

  Go Get a Scotch, Man, 69

  A Room with Vermouth, 49

  A Time to Swill, 88

vodka, 10

  Absolut, Absolut!, 54

  The Brothers Kamikaze, 47

David Copper Mug, 55

Drinker Tailor Soldier Spy, 73

Fifty Shades of Grey Goose, 60

The Hitchhiker's Mudslide to the Galaxy, 81

Nineteen Eighty-Forty, 70

War and Peas, 121

W

Waller, Robert James, *The Bridges of Madison County,* 118

War and Peace (Tolstoy), 121

War and Peas, 121

Watership Down (Adams), 101

Watership Down the Hatch, 101

Wells, H. G., *The Island of Dr. Moreau,* 23

whiskey, 10

  The Call of the Wild Turkey, 53

  The Drinking Game of Thrones, 75

  Extremely Drunk and Incredibly Close, 63

  Go Get a Scotch, Man, 69

  Goodnight Moonshine, 104

  The Hard Cider House Rules, 66

  As I Lay Drinking, 50

  Lord Jim Beam, 42

  Portrait of the Artist as a Drunk Man, 20

  The Seagram's Garden (spiked version), 108

Wilder, Laura Ingalls, *Little House on the Prairie,* 102

Wild Turkey bourbon, *in* The Call of the Wild Turkey, 53

The Wind in the Willows (Grahame), 95

wine, fortified wine, 12

The Bellini Jar, 84

Dangerous Libations, 44

David Copper Mug, 55

Extremely Drunk and Incredibly
Close, 63

Go Get a Scotch, Man, 69

The Island of Dr. Merlot, 23

Of Mice and Manischewitz, 41

A Room with Vermouth, 49

She Stoops to Cointreau, 26

Tender is the Nightcap, 18

The Tequila Sun Also Rises, 35

A Time to Swill, 88

The Wine in the Willows, 95

The Wine of Beauty, 79

Z

*Zen and the Art of Motorcycle
Maintenance* (Pirsig), 76